CB128314

NATURAL SCIENCE PRIMARY 6

BY ME

ACTIVITY BOOK

UNIT 1 Interaction

1 Read the sentences about the functions of the brain and answer the questions below.

- Different regions of the brain manage different functions.
- Vision and reading are controlled by the occipital lobe.
- The right hemisphere controls the left side of the body.
- The brain stem controls respiration among other vital functions.

a. Which hemisphere controls the right side of the body?

____

b. Which sense(s) does the occipital lobe control?

____

c. Which part of the brain controls breathing?

____

2 Label the parts of the brain.

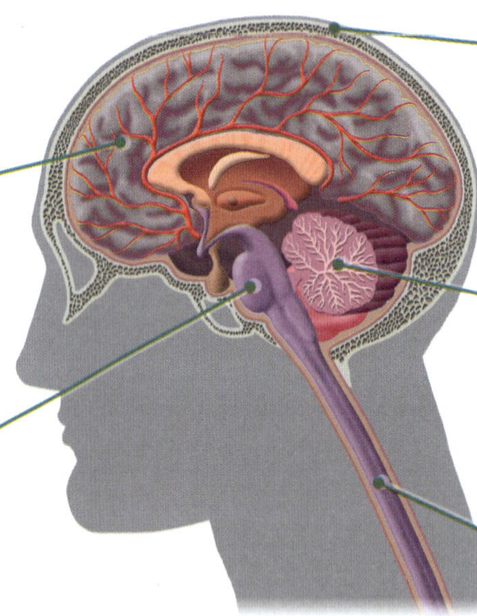

a. ______________

b. ______________

c. ______________

d. ______________

e. ______________

3 Decide whether the following sentences are true (T) or false (F).

a. The senses of smell and taste are related. ☐

b. The loss of our sense of smell is called anosmia. ☐

c. Your sense of smell declines when you reach 50. ☐

d. There are six basic tastes. ☐

4. Read the text about the sense of smell. What do the words or expressions in bold mean? Circle the correct meaning/synonym.

The process of smelling can easily be explained. Imagine something that smells quite strong, for example garlic. A molecule is released from this **fragrance** which stimulates special nerve cells in the nose. Once received, the information is **transmitted** to the brain and this impressive organ can **detect** the specific smell. The sense of smell can be affected by a number of different things, **e.g.** a cold or nerve damage. When this sense is affected, it also interferes with our ability to taste because our taste buds are limited in the number of flavours they can detect on their own.

1. fragrance
   a. odorous b. smell c. object
2. transmitted
   a. called b. sent c. thrown
3. detect
   a. identify b. picked c. ignore
4. e.g.
   a. therefore b. for example c. however

5. Umami is considered to be a fifth basic taste. Find out more about umami. Tick (✔) the foods that are rich in umami.

a. mushrooms ☐ d. chocolate ☐ g. tomatoes ☐
b. chicken ☐ e. soy ☐ h. milk ☐
c. beef ☐ f. salt ☐ i. pork ☐

6. Label the photos with the matching tastes.

a 
____

b 
____

umami
salty
bitter
sweet
sour

c 
____

d 
____

e 
____

7 Look at the following photos. Explain what each part of the body enables you to do and why it is important.

a
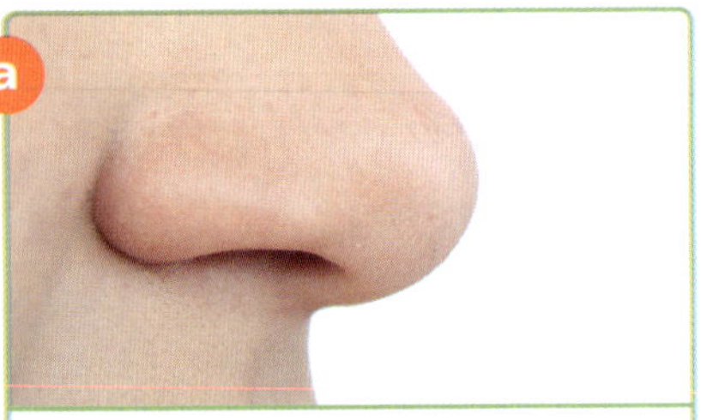

This enables me to smell different fragrances and is connected to taste, too. The sense of smell is important because

b
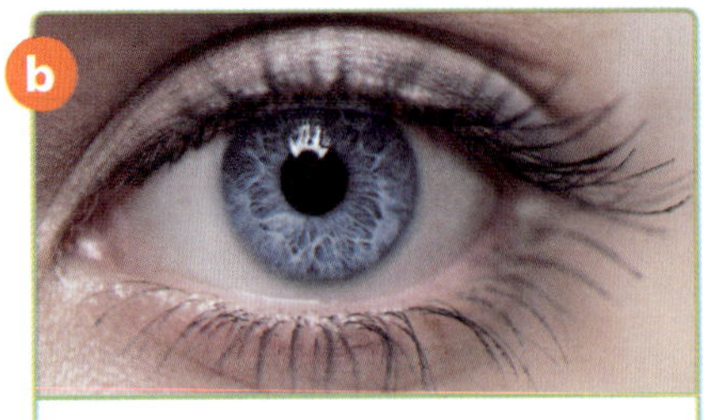

c
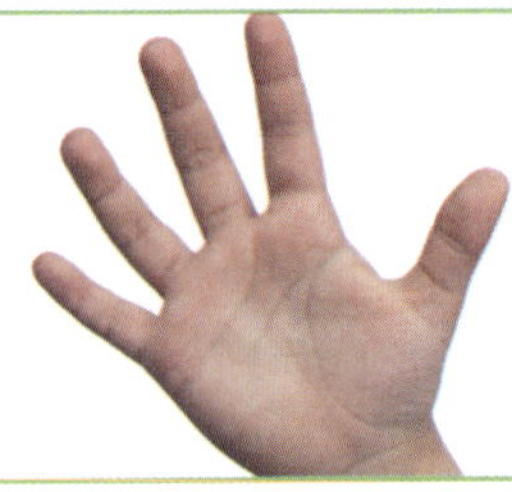

8 Imagine that you are a doctor. Give advice to a patient who is complaining of back pain. How can they keep their spine healthy?

Language for giving advice

- *You should / shouldn't ...*
- *You might want to ...*
- *What you could do is ...*

9 Label the picture by using the words from the box. There is one extra word.

clavicle	tibia	patella	scapula	sternum	radius	pelvis	humerus

a. ____________________

b. ____________________

c. ____________________

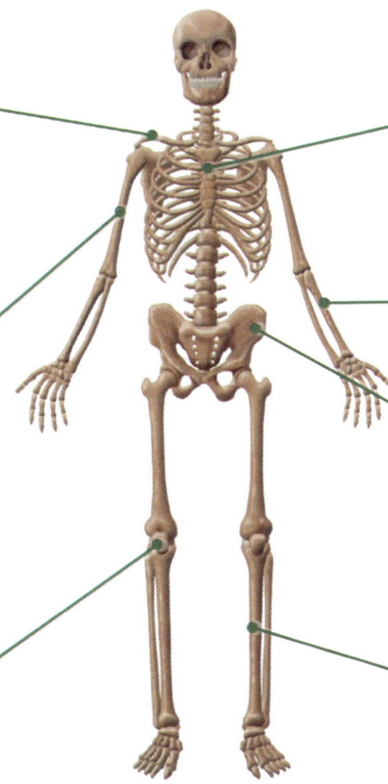

d. ____________________

e. ____________________

f. ____________________

g. ____________________

10 What muscles are they? Read the definitions and choose the correct muscle from the box.

pectoral muscle	deltoid	calf muscle	gluteus	biceps

a. ____________________: this muscle is found in the chest.

b. ____________________: this muscle pulls the heel up to allow movement in the leg.

c. ____________________: this muscle lies on the upper arm between the shoulder and the elbow.

d. ____________________: this muscle forms the rounded shape of the shoulder.

e. ____________________: this muscle is found in the buttocks.

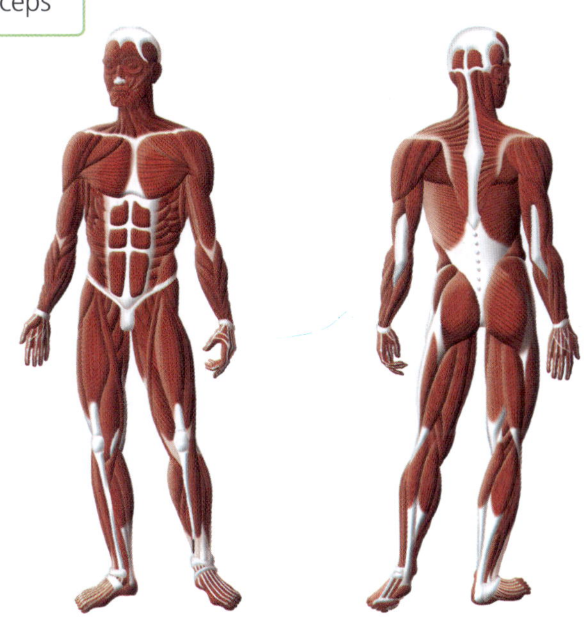

Project work

11 Think about the bodily changes that take place throughout your life. Complete the table with your ideas. Then, with a partner, think of two more types of change to add to the table and make notes about them.

	changes
the brain	
coordination	
bones and organs	
physical strength	

12 Compare your answers in small groups. Add other students' ideas to your table if they are different.

13 In the same small groups, organise your ideas visually. You can choose one of the options below or use your own method. Then, present your ideas to the class.

- a poster
- a leaflet
- a spider diagram
- a comic strip
- question and answer cards
- a mind map

Skills check

14 Read the text below about our senses. Choose the best word for each space.

Humans have a number of senses. The correct scientific names are only really (1) __________ by doctors or specialists. For example, we would normally say 'sight' (2) __________ the scientific term is 'ophthalmoception'.

The (3) __________ senses have scientific names, too. The senses are divided into external and internal senses. The first type are the traditional senses: sight, hearing, touch, taste and smell. The (4) __________ group consists of senses that are perceived from within the body such (5) __________ hunger and balance.

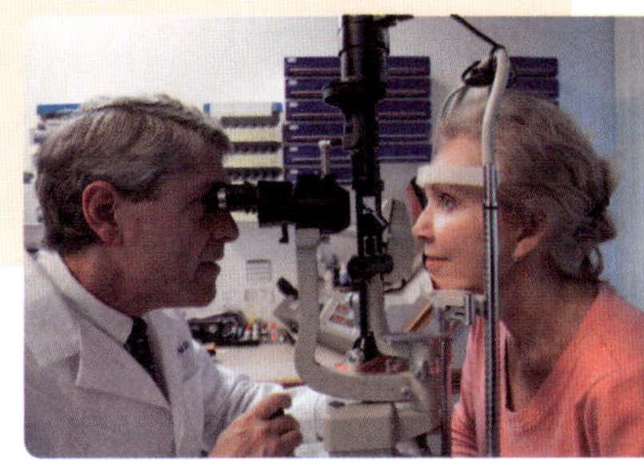

1. said / told / used / given
2. but / and / here / or
3. another / last / right / other
4. final / latter / before / aforementioned
5. like / when / of / as

15 Read the text about orthopaedics and then fill in each blank with one word from the box below. The first one has been done for you.

before	if	and	or	not	~~to~~	an	their

Orthopaedic doctors and surgeons diagnose and treat any condition that is related *to* the musculoskeletal system. The diseases and injuries that (1) __________ orthopaedic surgeon deals with include the following: arthritis, bone tumours, fractures, sprains (2) __________ dislocations. This is (3) __________ an exhaustive list – there are many more. People should see an orthopaedic doctor (4) __________ they are experiencing pain in (5) __________ ankles, knees, hips, shoulders (6) __________ back. Doctors in this field do everything they can to treat the condition with medicine and physical therapy (7) __________ resorting to surgery.

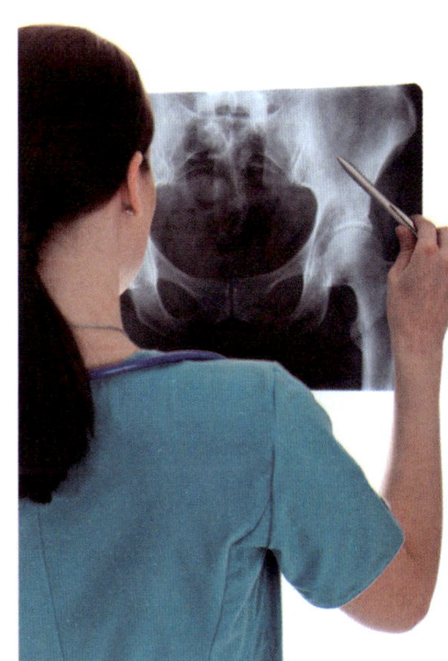

1. Decide whether the sentences are true (T) or false (F). Correct the false sentences.

a. The anus is part of the excretory system. ☐

____

b. The kidneys filter blood. ☐

____

c. The intestines are part of the respiratory system. ☐

____

d. The trachea aids in digestion. ☐

____

e. The stomach helps our circulation. ☐

____

2. Read the texts about different drugs. In each case, which drug is being referred to? Write the names and match the texts with the photos.

1. ______________ ☐
This drug affects our lungs and our respiratory system in general. It is a highly addictive substance that is extremely harmful. There are about 5 million deaths per year associated with this drug.

2. ______________ ☐
This drug can affect more than just our physical health. If abused, it can lead to brain abnormalities. Short-term effects of taking this drug include disorientation, rapid heartbeat and anxiety.

3. ______________ ☐
This drug dramatically affects the functioning of our liver. If not consumed moderately, it can lead to a lot of health problems. About 2.5 million people on average die from abusing this drug every single year.

a

b

c

3 Imagine you are a doctor giving written advice to patients about their digestive systems.

1. What happens if we don't look after our digestive system?

2. How can we look after our digestive system properly?

4 Read the information about how blood flows in the heart. Tick (✔) the correct sentences.

Blood flowing to the heart enters on the right side through two veins called the superior vena cava and the inferior vena cava. The superior vein collects the blood from the upper half of the body and the inferior vein from the lower half. Once the blood has left these veins, it enters the right atrium, which contracts and pushes blood down to the right ventricle. After further contraction, the blood is pushed into the lungs, where it collects oxygen. The blood flows through the lungs and then enters the heart through the left side. Next, it flows to the rest of the body.

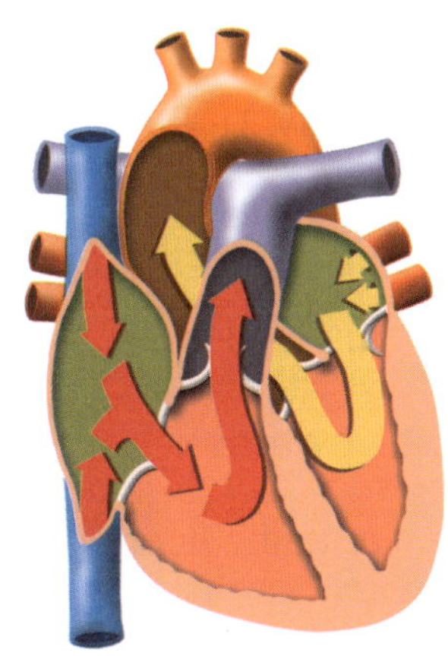

a. Oxygenated blood enters the left side of the heart. ☐

b. The inferior vena cava is a vein. ☐

c. The superior vena cava works with the lower part of the body. ☐

d. Blood is pushed into the respiratory organs. ☐

e. Blood picks up oxygen from the lungs. ☐

5 Explain, in your own words, the function of each component of blood.

a. ______________________________

____

b. ______________________________

____

c. ______________________________

____

d. ______________________________

____

6 Read about the diaphragm and its place within the respiratory system. What do the words or expressions in bold mean? Circle the words or phrases below that have the same meaning.

The diaphragm is made up of skeletal muscle. It is **dome-shaped** and is curved **upwards**. It separates the heart and lungs from the abdominal cavity. It **plays a huge role in** respiration. It is surrounded by arteries and veins above and below. These arteries and veins **supply** and drain blood.

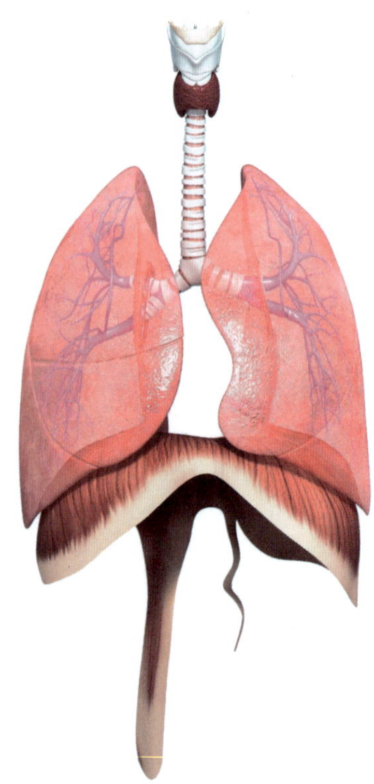

1. dome-shaped
   - a. rounded
   - b. square
   - c. triangular
2. upwards
   - a. to the floor
   - b. to the ceiling
   - c. across
3. plays a huge role in
   - a. is related to
   - b. is active in
   - c. is based on
4. role
   - a. part
   - b. tool
   - c. key
5. supply
   - a. enter
   - b. provide
   - c. get

7 Write about how we can look after our respiratory system.

We should ...

We shouldn't ...

8 Sweating is very good for us. Can you give three reasons why?

a.

b.

c.

9 Name the organs shown below. Say which systems they each belong to, and explain their role.

a 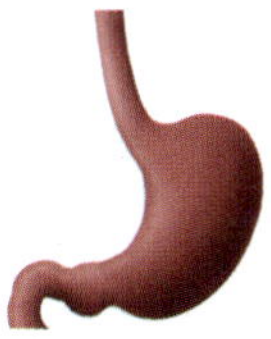

stomach:

b 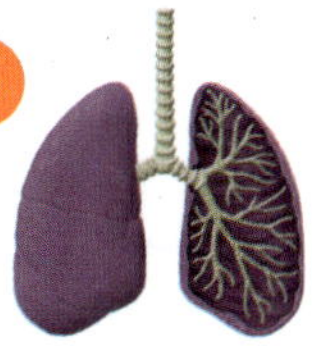

c 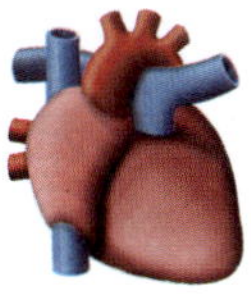

Project work

10 Look at the shopping lists below, which were written by three different people. Decide if the lists are *healthy, unhealthy* or *in need of improvement.* Underline the unhealthy items in the lists.

Person 1:	Person 2:	Person 3:
____________	____________	____________
• celery	• sweets	• orange juice
• bananas	• crisps	• pizza
• strawberries	• popcorn	• carrots
• green apples	• ham	• kiwis
• bar of chocolate	• jam	• grapes
• brown rice	• white bread	• brown rice
• pasta	• white rice	• white bread

11 Write some advice to the person above who has the unhealthy shopping list. Then create a new and interesting shopping list for them.

Tell them:

a. why their diet is unhealthy.

b. what they should eat instead.

c. what they should eat for a typical breakfast, lunch and dinner.

A new shopping list:

Skills check

12 Read the facts about the digestive system and correct the underlined grammar or vocabulary mistakes.

The digestive system has two main functions: to rid the body (1) off waste and to convert food into (2) nutriants for the body. The small intestine is where most of the digestion takes place. It absorbs the nutrients and passes them (3) too the bloodstream. Bacteria (4) is killed by hydrochloric acid secreted (5) for the cells on the inner walls of the stomach. This acid is also found in some cleaning products.

Some animals have (6) know stomach, for example seahorses and platypuses. (7) They food goes straight from the (8) osophagus to the intestines.

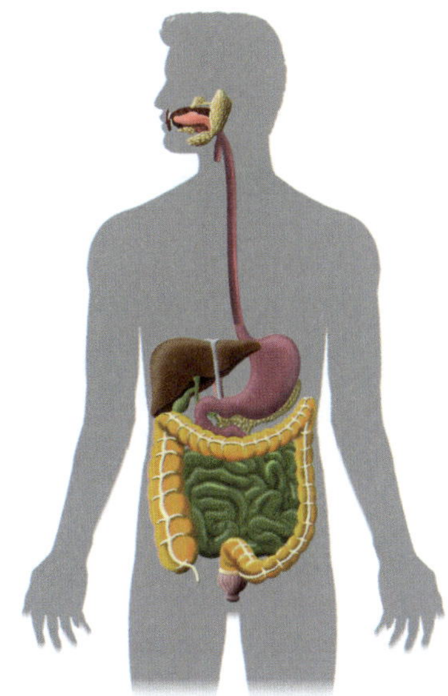

1. ____________
2. ____________
3. ____________
4. ____________
5. ____________
6. ____________
7. ____________
8. ____________

13 Read about the importance of the excretory system and choose the best word for each space.

Our urinary system is (1) ____________ important because it eliminates waste from the body. Some of this waste (2) ____________ be potentially toxic and hence harmful to us. The kidneys (3) ____________ ureters play an important role in this system. The kidneys take in water and chemicals, (4) ____________ a large portion is returned to the blood. Other organs that are important to the excretory system are the liver and skin, (5) ____________ are actively involved in removing toxic and waste materials via sweating.

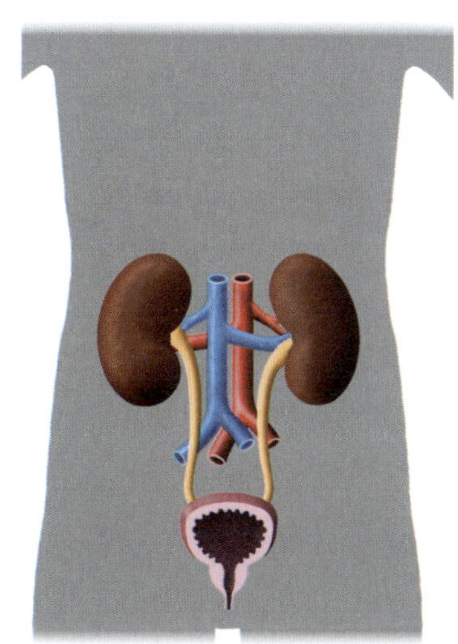

1. not / so / huge / little
2. may / is / would / definitely
3. or / and / because / too
4. but / so / and / where
5. where / what / when / which

UNIT 3 Reproduction

1 Read the information about elderly people. Then read the sentences below and tick (✔) the correct ones.

There is a natural reduction in the capacity of a person's biological system as they age. This rate of decline can depend on many factors related to lifestyle, environment and genetic predisposition. Lifestyle and environmental factors are those related to our diet, exercise and exposure to harmful or toxic substances, such as smoke, alcohol and drugs.

People are living longer in general and as a result there is also an increase in the number of people living with dementia, a progressive disorder affecting how the brain works and what a person remembers. However, getting dementia is not a certain consequence of growing old.

a. Old age does not affect biological capacity. ☐

b. Lifestyle and environment are the only factors related to biological capacity. ☐

c. Alcohol and drug consumption can affect our biological systems. ☐

d. Life expectancy is increasing. ☐

e. Dementia is a typical consequence of old age. ☐

2 Write comparative sentences about the differences between males and females in relation to the following:

a. hips

Female hips are generally wider than male hips.

b. hair

______

c. life expectancy

______

d. muscles

______

e. lungs

______

3 Label the pictures. Then, write the definitions.

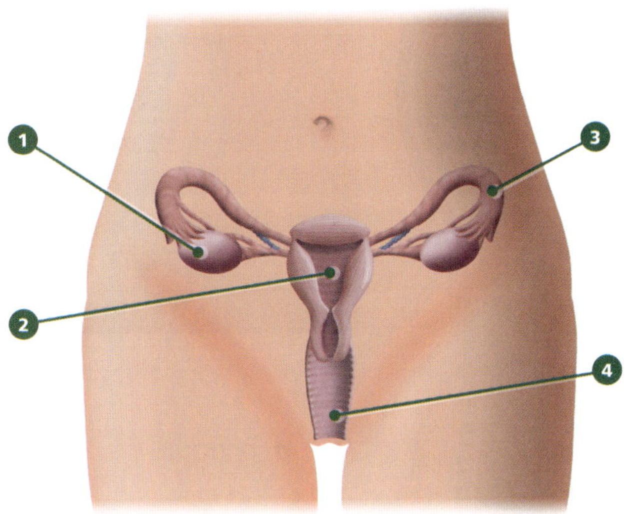

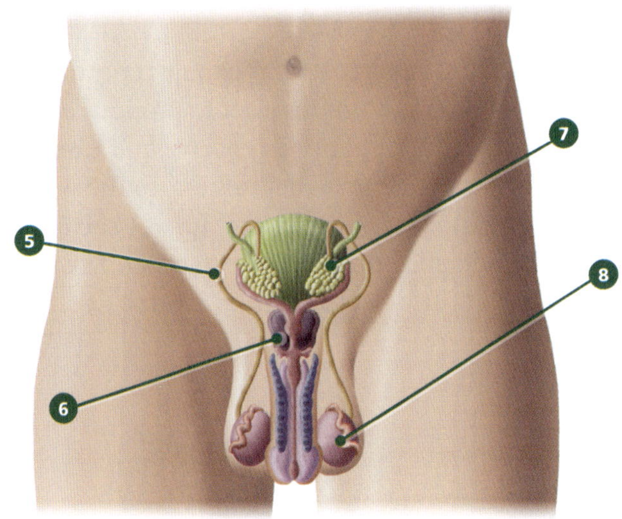

1. *Ovaries: They produce female sex cells called ova.*
2. ______
3. ______
4. ______
5. ______
6. ______
7. ______
8. ______

4 Put the stages of the menstrual cycle in order.

- [ ] The ovaries produce an egg.
- [ ] If the egg is not fertilised, it dries up.
- [ ] The egg leaves the body through the vagina.
- [ ] The egg leaves the ovary.
- [ ] The walls of the uterus prepare for fertilisation by getting thicker.
- [ ] The egg moves into one of the fallopian tubes.

5 Read the information about the male reproductive system. What do the words in bold mean? Circle the words or phrases below that have the same meaning.

The **main** purpose of the male reproductive system is to fertilise a woman's ovum in order to produce a baby. This is done through the production, **maintenance** and transportation of sperm and a protective fluid, called semen, to the woman's ovum. The scrotum is the organ that **houses** the testicles, which are responsible for sperm production. The male reproductive system maintains itself by producing and **secreting** male sex hormones.

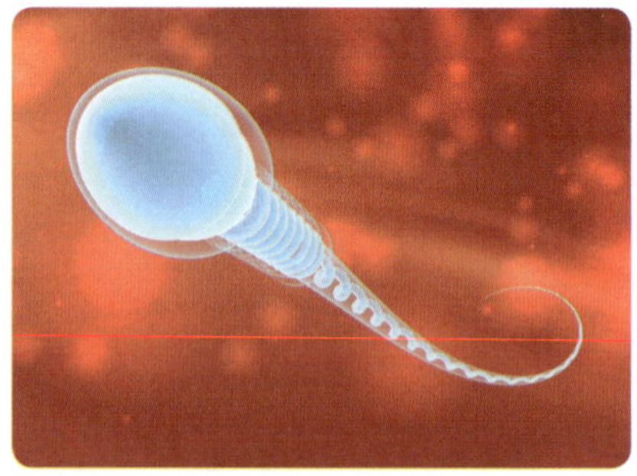

1. main

   a. big b. small c. large d. principal

2. maintenance

   a. preservation b. relax c. relief d. carry

3. houses

   a. cares for b. accustoms c. watches d. holds

4. secreting

   a. emitting b. observing c. transporting d. smelling

6 Find out more about puberty. Write about the differences between boys and girls in puberty. Use the following headings to help you.

1. age of puberty

____

____

2. first signs of puberty

____

____

3. weight changes

____

____

7 Put the stages of pregnancy in order and label the pictures with the words from the box.

zygote (x3)	foetus	embryo	fertilisation

a

☐ ____________________

b

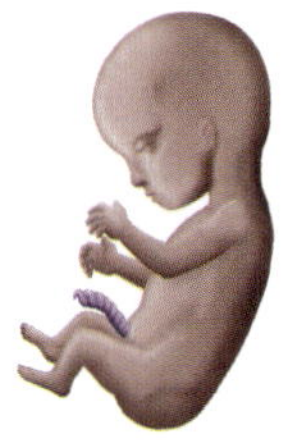

☐ ____________________

c

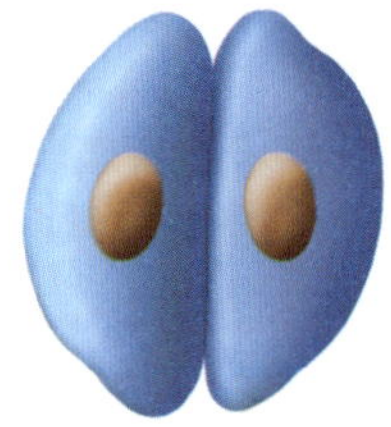

☐ ____________________

d

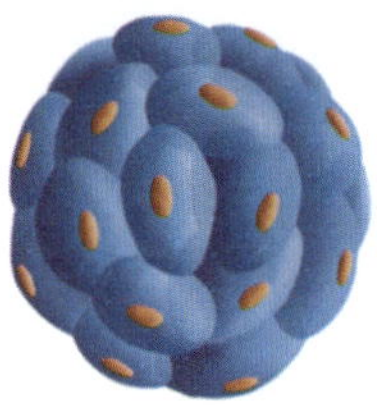

☐ ____________________

e

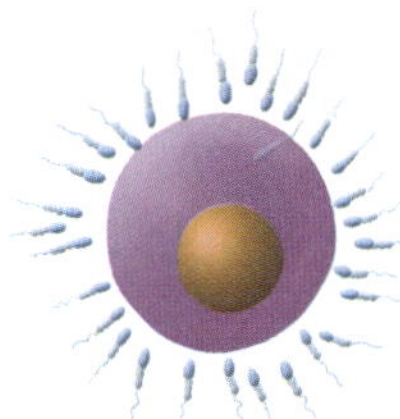

☐ ____________________

f

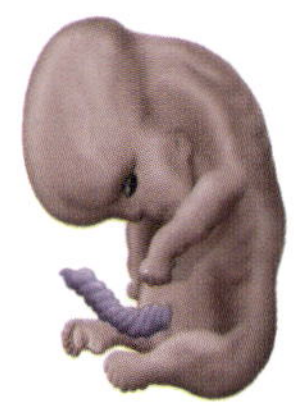

☐ ____________________

8 Read about the third trimester in pregnancy and decide whether the sentences below are true (T) or false (F).

The third trimester signals the end of a pregnancy. At the end of a pregnancy, foetal development continues. By about week 28, the eyes are partially open and the eyelashes are formed. The baby also gains weight, which smooths out wrinkles in the skin. The baby's bones are fully developed, but are still soft and flexible. Even though the lungs aren´t fully formed, breathing is practised. In week 31, the nervous system starts to control temperature regulation. Soon after, the baby's pupils can constrict, dilate and detect light.

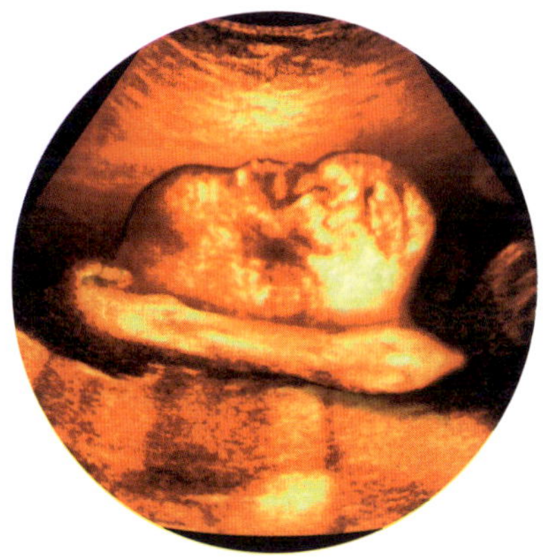

a. The third trimester is the last stage of pregnancy. ☐

b. The eyes are completely open at the beginning of this stage. ☐

c. The baby's bones are rigid. ☐

d. The baby cannot see anything. ☐

e. The baby's lungs are fully developed. ☐

f. The baby's eyes cannot detect light. ☐

Project work

9 Have you ever thought about the differences between adolescents, adults and elderly people? What differences do you think might exist?

Method

1. Find three people to test: an adolescent, an adult and an elderly person over 75.
2. Complete three tests and record the results in the table below. Analyse the differences.

Test

1. Give each person 10 details (for example, words, sentences, or pictures) to remember at the beginning of the test.
2. Ask them to rate their flexibility from 1 to 10.
3. Ask them to perform the 'sit and reach test' (see the photo on the right) and measure the distance in centimetres.
4. Ask them to remember the 10 details.

	memory test (1-10)	self-assessment of flexibility (1-10)	flexibility test (cm)
adolescent			
adult			
elderly person			

Conclusions

1. What differences did you find?

____

____

2. Why do you think these differences exist?

____

____

3. Can we do anything to avoid these differences? What could you do to improve your memory and flexibility?

____

____

Skills check

10 Read the text about UNICEF. Choose the correct word for each space.

UNICEF, the United Nations Children's Fund, (1) ____________ a global organisation that provides long-term assistance (2) ____________ children and mothers in developing countries. They believe that children should be given the best start in life and that proper care is the (3) ____________ important thing a person can give their child. They are there to help create a solid foundation for every child that needs one.

The organisation was founded in 1946 and its headquarters are in New York, USA. UNICEF works all (4) ____________ the world and is active in more (5) ____________ 190 countries.

UNICEF promotes female education up to at least the end of primary level. It (6) ____________ focuses on child survival and development, basic education, gender equality and child protection. The needs of each country or territory (7) ____________ identified and UNICEF provides the necessary assistance.

One of UNICEF's child protection projects aims to change social norms relating to forms of violence and abuse which are considered socially acceptable. UNICEF continues to do great work (8) ____________ governments in order to improve laws.

1. is / it / with / since

2. on / of / in / to

3. less / more / most / big

4. over / in / on / for

5. that / than / up / less

6. in addition / plus / also / to

7. is / are / so / were

8. on / with / in / of

11 Read the text in Activity 10 again. Write the definitions for these words.

a. headquarters: ______________________________

____

b. gender equality: ______________________________

____

c. law: ______________________________

____

UNIT 4

Living things

1 Match the photos to the correct words and write their definitions.

1

2

3

4

5

6

a. respiration ☐

____

____

b. excretion ☐

____

____

c. nutrition ☐

____

____

d. interaction ☐

____

____

e. growth ☐

____

____

f. reproduction ☐

____

____

2 Decide whether the following things are living or non-living and write each word in the correct column. Then add two examples of your own to each column.

an icicle | a rock
a mushroom | a river
a coral | fire
a cat | a cell
a seed | a cloud
a clock | a volcano
bubbles | bacteria
a sunflower

living things	non-living things

3 Read the text about plant and animal cells, then decide whether the sentences below are true (**T**) or false (**F**).

All organisms are composed of cells. Cells are the basic structural and functional units of life. The general structures of plant cells and animal cells are the same, for example they both have a nucleus, the 'boss' of the cell. This is where the cell's genetic material is found. However, there are some key differences between these cells.

Animal cells can change their shape unlike plant cells, which have a cell wall. The main function of a cell wall is to provide protection and to regulate activity from the inside to the outside, and vice versa.

Plants use photosynthesis, which takes place in their chloroplasts, whereas animal cells don't have these structures. Mitochondria are like power stations as they create energy. In both types of cell they break down sugar and convert it into energy.

a. The structures of plant and animal cells are quite similar. ☐

b. Animal cells have a cell wall. ☐

c. Plant cell energy is produced in chloroplasts. ☐

d. Only animal cells have mitochondria. ☐

4 What is the main responsibility of each of these organelles found in both plant and animal cells? Write one sentence for each organelle and draw a picture of it.

a nucleus

b mitochondria

c vacuole

d cell membrane

5. Read the sentences. Which kingdom does each one describe?

a. Organisms in this kingdom perform photosynthesis, which is the conversion of light energy into chemical energy. Other life forms depend on this kingdom. ______

b. Organisms in this kingdom, such as bacteria, usually exist as single cells with no nucleus.

______

c. Organisms in this kingdom, such as amoebae, are larger than bacteria but only have one cell.

______

d. Organisms in this kingdom are classified into vertebrates and invertebrates.

______

e. Organisms in this kingdom are involved in the decomposition of organic matter.

______

6. Which kingdoms do these organisms belong to? Label the photos. Some photos show organisms from more than one kingdom.

a

______

______

b
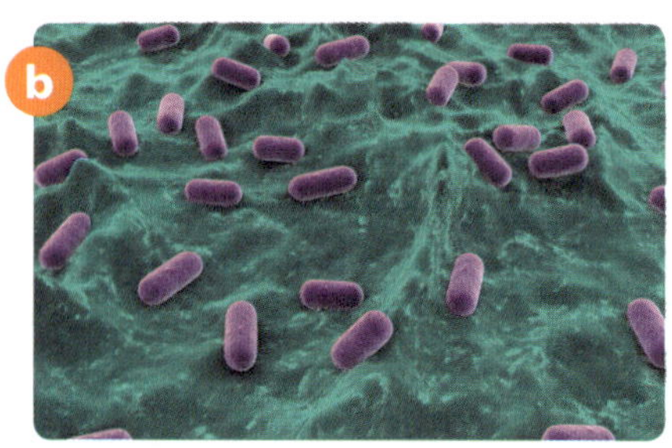

______

______

c

______

______

d

______

______

e

______

______

f
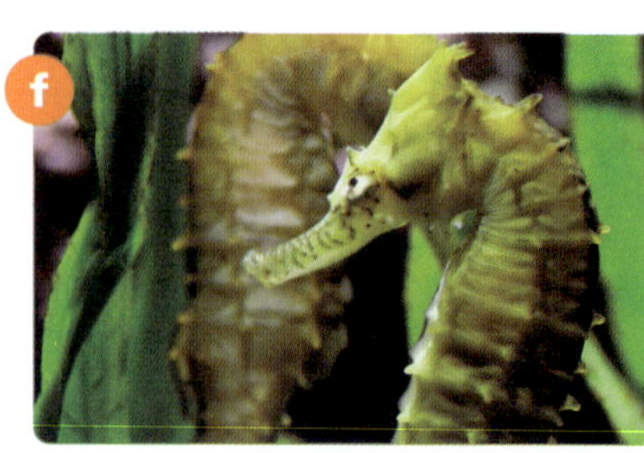

______

______

7. Read the following sentences about photosynthesis and decide whether they are true (**T**) or false (**F**). Correct the false ones.

a. Photosynthesis is the process in which fungi transform energy from the Sun. ☐

____

b. All organisms require energy to carry out life processes. ☐

____

c. Plants absorb oxygen and release carbon dioxide. ☐

____

d. Plants make their own food during the process of reproduction. ☐

____

e. Oxygen is released into the air as a result of photosynthesis. ☐

____

8. Find out more about photosynthesis. Write about the advantages of this process in relation to the four topics below.

1. medicines

____

____

2. energy

____

____

3. the environment

____

____

4. food

____

____

Project work

9 Do certain colours of light change the way plants grow? How important is light for photosynthesis? You are going to observe and record plant growth in different types of light over a period of three weeks.

Materials

- potting soil
- plant seeds of your choice
- red-, green-, blue-, and yellow-coloured cellophane
- ordinary tap water
- 4 planting trays

Method

1. Plant the seeds (according to the instructions on the seed packet) in each of the four trays.
2. Cover each tray with a piece of different coloured cellophane.
3. Record the height (in centimetres) of the plants each week for each of the four colours.
4. Note down any differences in the appearance of the plants for each colour.

	week 1	week 2	week 3
red			
green			
blue			
yellow			

Conclusions

1. Does the colour of the light affect plant growth?

2. What else affects how plants grow?

Skills check

10 Read the text about the history of taxonomy. Then decide whether the sentences below are true (**T**) or false (**F**).

Taxonomy is the term used to describe the classification of organisms. There are billions of organisms that have existed or still exist on Earth. Some of them are extinct, others have evolved and only a small percentage of them are around today.

Taxonomy is the systematic classification of organisms based on their similarities. A person who is a specialist in this field is called a taxonomist. The classification of organisms has many advantages, not least because the system helps to prevent living things being given misnomers. This is achieved by allocating a homogeneous name to an organism. This means that everyone who uses the system can understand precisely which organism is being referred to.

The first taxonomist, Aristotle, divided animals into those with blood and those without blood. In the field of botany, John Ray was another early taxonomist who devised a system which gave long descriptions to plants. These older systems required some modifications, which is where the 18th century taxonomist Carl Linnaeus comes in. He is often referred to as the father of modern taxonomy due to his classification of organisms based on their structures.

Modern classification takes into account internal and external structures, where organisms live, and their breeding behaviour.

a. Taxonomy is a system of naming and classifying living things. ☐

b. The first taxonomist divided animals into four groups. ☐

c. Botany is related to plant and animal study. ☐

d. The earlier systems of taxonomy were complete. ☐

e. Carl Linnaeus classified organisms according to their structure among other things. ☐

f. Geography and reproduction methods are important elements in modern classification. ☐

11 Read the text in Activity 10 again. Write definitions for the words below.

a. extinct: ______________________

b. misnomer: ______________________

c. botany: ______________________

d. breeding: ______________________

UNIT 5 Ecosystems

1. Look at the photos. Name the different ecosystems and give the names of two organisms that live in each one.

a 

b 

c 

d 

e 

f 

2. Read the text about fish in the Arctic and then decide whether the sentences below are true (T) or false (F).

How some fish can survive in the Arctic Ocean had scientists confused for a while. The waters in which the fish live are extremely cold, which means that these species have to adapt in some way. When temperatures reach a certain low point, ice crystals form in the organisms' cells. In theory, this should cause irreversible damage to the organisms that live there and perhaps even death. However, scientists have found out why fish in the Arctic can thrive in this environment. The reason for this is an antifreeze protein in their blood, which permits survival.

a. Scientists were confused by the survival of fish in the Arctic. ☐

b. Fish in the Arctic do the opposite to what is expected: they don't die. ☐

c. A special protein helps them stay alive. ☐

3 Choose the correct words from the box that best fit the definitions below.

community	ecosystem	population	habitat
organism	kingdom	grassland	tundra

a. A taxonomic rank which groups together different forms of life: ____________________

b. A group of animals and plants that live together: ____________________

c. An ecosystem with very low temperatures: ____________________

d. The place where an organism lives: ____________________

4 Write the missing definitions from Activity 3.

a. ______________: ____

b. ______________: ____

c. ______________: ____

d. ______________: ____

5 Find out more about tropical rainforests. Write three examples of fauna and flora for each layer.

	fauna	flora
emergent layer		
canopy layer		
understory layer		
forest floor		

6 Rewrite the sentences about food chains and food webs so that they are correct.

a. There are five levels in a food chain.

____

b. Herbivores (organisms that only eat plants) are also called autotrophs.

____

c. Tertiary consumers feed on dead organic matter.

____

d. A food web is the food which is available for the next trophic level.

____

e. There is more biomass at the higher levels of a food web.

____

7 Complete the text using the words from the box.

bottom	Sun	grass	trees	middle
predators	herbivores	prey	deer	rabbits

At the (1) ________ of the food chain are plants such as (2) ________ and (3) ________. They get their energy from the (4) ________. In the (5) ________ of the food chain are animals such as (6) ________ and (7) ________. These animals eat plants and are called (8) ________.

The top of the food chain includes animals such as lions and wolves. These animals are (9) ________, because they eat other animals. The animals that they eat are (10) ________ for the predators.

8 Read the sentences about biodiversity. What do the words in bold mean? Circle the correct meanings.

1. Biodiversity is the variety of **organisms** in different ecosystems.

   a. beings b. life c. organs

2. Tropical regions contain a **large** percentage of the Earth's plant and animal species.

   a. small b. significant c. wide

3. Climate change is a big **threat** to biodiversity.

   a. hazard b. friend c. relation

4. Scientists **calculate** that about 8.7 million species have been discovered so far.

   a. say b. estimate c. claim

9 Imagine you are giving a presentation on biodiversity. Write some notes on the following:

a. Why is it important?

____

____

____

b. How is it being damaged?

____

____

____

c. How can we protect it?

____

____

____

Project work

10 What do you know about endangered species? Find out some interesting facts about endangered species and write them down.

a. *A species is endangered when its habitat is damaged or when it is a victim of a disease or predation.*

b. ______

c. ______

d. ______

e. ______

f. ______

11 Learn about a specific endangered species in a different part of the world and answer the questions.

What is the name of the endangered species? What does it look like?	
What are some interesting facts related to this species?	
What ecosystem does it live in?	
What does it eat?	
Is it prey, predator or both?	
Why is it under threat?	
Is there anything being done to protect it?	
What else could be done?	

12 Take action by creating a presentation or poster which illustrates your research.

Skills check

13 Write the definitions for the following words.

a. biomass (*noun*): ______

b. carnivore (*noun*): ______

c. omnivore (*noun*): ______

d. endangered (*adjective*): ______

e. extinct (*adjective*): ______

f. evolve (*verb*): ______

g. threaten (*verb*): ______

14 Write an email.

A friend has emailed you asking for your help with a presentation about an ecosystem. Write an email to your friend. In your email you should:

- Say thanks for their email.
- Tell your friend how pleased you are to help.
- Answer any of your friend's questions after finding out about the ecosystem.
- Give your friend some advice on how to organise the presentation.

Dear ______

UNIT 6 Matter

1. Match the words to the correct definitions.

1. matter
2. a homogeneous mixture
3. a pure substance
4. a heterogeneous mixture
5. a mixture

a. a substance made up of at least two different pure substances
b. a type of mixture that is made up of two substances which keep their own properties
c. anything that occupies space and has particles
d. a type of mixture that is uniform in composition
e. a material that only has one type of particle

2. Look at the photos and label the substances using words from Activity 1.

a

____

b

____

c

____

3. Explain the following terms.

a. volume: ______________________
b. density: ______________________
c. mass: ______________________
d. irreversible change: ______________________
e. reversible change: ______________________

4 Find out more about salt. Tick (✔) the correct sentences.

a. Every cell in the body contains salt. ☐

b. The chemical symbol for salt is NaCl. ☐

c. Delineation is the extraction of salt from water. ☐

d. The chemical name for salt is sodium chloride. ☐

e. Salt is not a pure substance. ☐

5 Read about the uses of salt, then circle the correct words in the sentences below.

Salt is all around us. It is one of the most abundant and useful minerals on Earth. As far as our bodies are concerned, salt regulates our water content so we don't dehydrate. Salt is present in most foods in small quantities and is added by chefs to most dishes as it is thought to bring out other flavours. The biggest use of salt, coming in at around 70 per cent, is for industrial chemicals. It is used in the chemical industry as a source of chlorine, not least because it has antiseptic properties. Around 10 per cent of salt is used for water conditioning and the rest for agricultural uses and de-icing roads.

a. Salt is a *mineral / solution*.

b. It helps us to keep *hydrated / dehydrated*.

c. About *10 per cent / 70 per cent* of salt is used in the chemical industry.

d. Salt *has / doesn't have* antiseptic properties.

e. Salt is also used in *agriculture / forestry*.

6 Read the text in Activity 5 again. Find synonyms of the words and phrases below.

1. balances: ______________________

2. appears: ______________________

3. more than enough: ______________________

4. to be without water: ______________________

5. preventing infection: ______________________

7 Look at the objects in the photos. Which separation method do you associate each of them with? Label them with the options from the box. There are some extra options.

decantation	evaporation	filtration	distillation	magnetic separation

a 

____

b 

____

c 

____

8 Identify the correct type of separation method mentioned in Activity 7.

a. This process boils something down to its most important part.

____

b. This process extracts material from a mixture using a type of force.

____

c. This process removes a layer of liquid from a mixture.

____

d. This process removes a solid from a mixture.

____

9 What type of method would you use to separate the following substances?

a. ground coffee from water: ______________________

b. paper clips from rubber bands: ______________________

c. salt from seawater: ______________________

d. sand from water: ______________________

e. water from alcohol: ______________________

f. iron filings from sand: ______________________

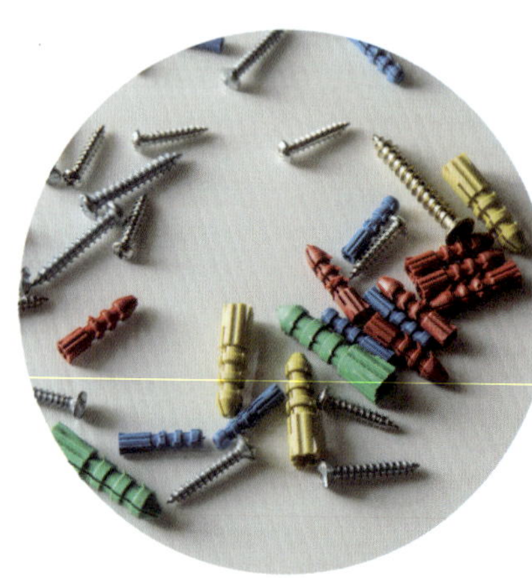

10 Read the sentences about the fermentation of wine and decide if they are true (T) or false (F). Correct the false ones.

a. During fermentation, oxygen is produced. ☐

____

b. Louis Pasteur investigated fermentation in the 20th century. ☐

____

c. People who are responsible for the fermentation process aren't concerned with flavour. ☐

____

d. Stainless steel vats are used to control fermentation temperatures. ☐

____

e. The yeast produced during fermentation turns the sugars into ethanol. ☐

____

f. Bacteria and amoebae are necessary in the fermentation process. ☐

____

11 Describe the process of fermentation in your own words.

a. Give a definition.

____

____

b. Explain the process.

____

____

____

c. Give an example.

____

____

Project work

12 What happens when food is exposed to oxygen? You are going to observe and record the process of oxidation over a week.

Materials

- a wedge (piece) of apple, potato and pear
- a plate

Observation

- What does the food look like each day?

	day 1	day 2	day 3	day 4	day 5	day 6	day 7
apple							
potato							
pear							

Conclusions

1. Were there any differences in the process of oxidation?

2. What are the dangers of eating oxidised food?

Skills check

13. Read the text about sugar and match the headings to the paragraphs.

Where is sugar found?	Is sugar really good for us?
What is sugar?	What are the dangers of sugars?

____

Sugar can be part of a balanced diet even though it has been linked to tooth decay. There has been no research as yet to suggest that it causes problems to our health if it is eaten in moderation, as is the case with a lot of food.

____

Sugar is a carbohydrate and can be further classified into two different types of sugar: monosaccharides and disaccharides. Glucose and fructose are examples of the former type.

____

Sugars such as glucose, fructose and lactose are found in a variety of foods. Glucose can be found in fruit, vegetables and cereal. Fructose is the main component of table sugar, while lactose is present in milk products.

____

Even though sugar is thought to be safe in moderate quantities, it can still cause problems. Many unhealthy foods contain added sugars. These can contribute to obesity, and, as a result, heart disease. Therefore, the majority of our calories should come from healthier, purer foods such as fruit and vegetables, which contain natural sugars and are a very good way to keep our bodies and teeth healthy.

14. Read the text from Activity 13 again. Decide whether the sentences below are true (**T**) or false (**F**).

a. Sugar is not bad for our teeth. ☐

b. Glucose is a monosaccharide. ☐

c. Lactose can be found in yoghurt. ☐

d. Glucose is not contained in vegetables. ☐

e. Unhealthy food often contains added sugars. ☐

15. Think of the things that you eat every day. List the foods that contain sugar. Do you think you eat too much sugar?

____

UNIT 7 Energy

1. Read the text about the advantages and disadvantages of non-renewable energy sources. What do the words and expressions in bold mean? Circle their synonyms.

Non-renewable energy means the energy comes from a source that will **run out** in the future. Examples of such energy sources are coal, oil and natural gas. In some cases, plants and trees are also classified as non-renewable sources **due to** deforestation. The fact that they **currently** seem to be widely available and reasonably affordable is one advantage of using non-renewable sources **such as** coal and oil. Another upside of using non-renewable sources is that extracting them is relatively cost-effective, which explains why oil and diesel, for example, are so readily available.

1. run out
   a. decrease b. disappear c. rise
2. due to
   a. as a result of b. like c. similar to
3. currently
   a. recently b. at the moment c. in the past
4. such as
   a. regarding b. related to c. like

2. What are some disadvantages of using non-renewable energy sources? Write about each disadvantage.

a

Land pollution: ______________________

b

Air pollution: ______________________

c

The future: ______________________

3 Provide a definition and give examples for each type of energy below.

1. heat energy
   - definition: ______________________________
   - examples: ______________________________
2. mechanical energy
   - definition: ______________________________
   - examples: ______________________________
3. chemical energy
   - definition: ______________________________
   - examples: ______________________________
4. electrical energy
   - definition: ______________________________
   - examples: ______________________________

4 List some benefits and dangers of the different energy forms below. Then match them to the photos.

	chemical energy	mechanical energy	potential energy	electrical energy
✔				
✘				
photo				

1 

2 

3 

4 

5 Classify the words below.

melting refraction colour insulator prism conduction
energy the Sun expansion conductor reflection transparent
radiation opaque convection evaporation translucent lens

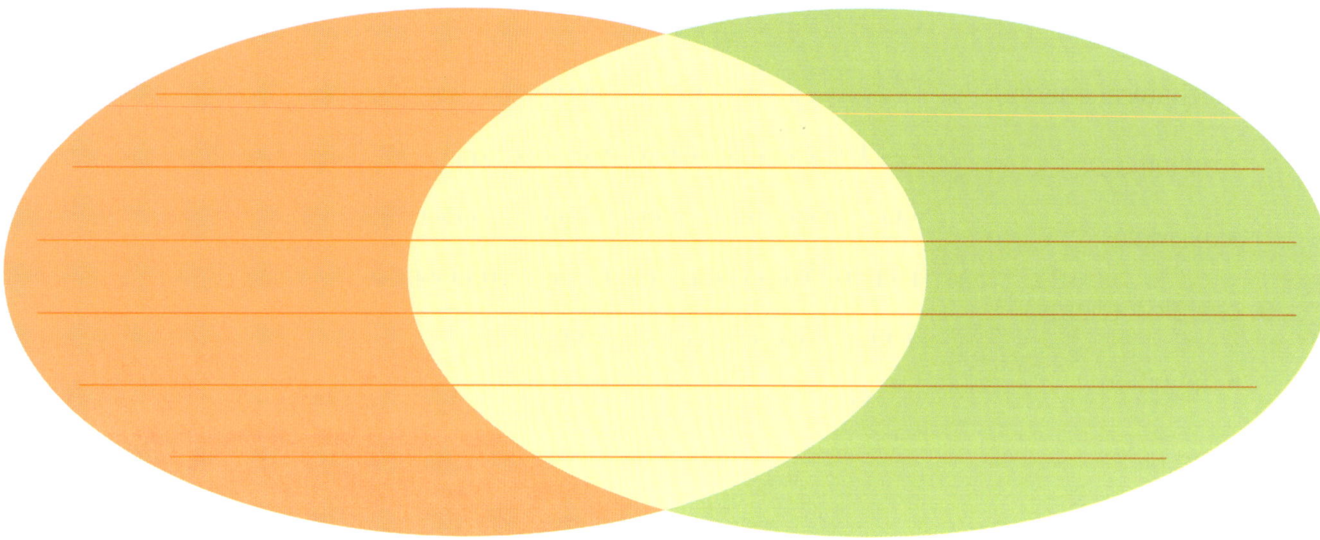

light heat

6 Explain the following terms.

a. conduction: ______________________________

____

b. radiation: ______________________________

____

c. convection: ______________________________

____

d. refraction: ______________________________

____

e. reflection: ______________________________

____

f. expansion: ______________________________

____

7 **Read the sentences about light. Correct the underlined grammar, vocabulary and punctuation mistakes. Rewrite the sentences.**

a. Light <u>move</u> extremely fast.

____

b. Light travels at different rates through different mediums <u>such glass</u>, water and air.

____

c. Photosynthesis is a <u>proces</u> whereby plants use energy <u>off</u> the sunlight to create chemical energy.

____

d. Light <u>is kind</u> of electromagnetic energy.

____

e. Sunlight can reach an ocean <u>deep</u> of 80 metres.

____

8 **Read the sentences. Which heat sources do they refer to? There are some extra sources in the box.**

the Sun	the Earth's core
a toaster	a car radiator
lightning	the human body
a full bathtub	a computer

a. This generates heat to warm us up and is the biggest source of heat energy in the Solar System.

____

b. The heat contained in this heat source can melt ice on the other side of a windscreen.

____

c. The heat contained in this source can start a natural fire or cause an electrical problem.

____

d. The energy contained in this source is stored underground and can heat buildings and produce electricity.

____

Project work

9 Have you ever thought about how much energy we waste? Have you ever thought about the negative effects this could have on the planet?

Materials

1. Think about the different activities you do every day. Make a list. How many of them involve using energy?
2. Look at the table below. What can you do to avoid wasting energy? Write some ideas. Add one more category and some energy-saving ideas for it.
3. Make a conscious effort to do all the activities that you listed every day. At the end of the week, tick the activities you have done at least once every day for that week. Hopefully you will incorporate them into your lifestyle naturally after this.

	day 1	day 2	day 3	day 4	day 5	day 6	day 7
water *I can turn the tap off while I'm brushing my teeth.*							
electrical appliances __________							
light __________							
air conditioning __________							
cleaning devices __________							
__________ __________							

Conclusions

1. What other devices waste a lot of energy? __________
2. What positive effect are you having on the world by completing a task like this? __________

____

Skills check

10 Read the text about energy saving on a hot day. Then decide if the sentences below are true (**T**) or false (**F**).

Hot weather can trigger an increase in energy usage, which is why it is important to know how to deal with this in a cost-effective way. There are many ways in which you can save energy, even when the Sun is shining, you are hot and you think you need to turn on the air conditioning. Here are some top tips:

- Make sure your air conditioner is in the best possible place. It should be placed so it can provide maximum potential for ventilation around the house. If you have ventilation fans in the bathroom or kitchen, you should turn them off 10 minutes after finishing cooking or taking a shower. You do not need them on any longer.
- The time of day is also important when it comes to saving energy. Things that make the house warmer, such as cooking or doing the laundry, should be done when it's cooler early in the morning or very late at night, for example. When you do cook, why not do it outside on a barbecue that uses less energy than a stove? Barbecues are also a lot of fun!
- You should take advantage of the weather by enjoying an afternoon by the pool or in the park. You do not have to be stuck at home increasing your energy bill when you could be enjoying your natural surroundings instead. When you do eventually arrive back home, you should also take advantage of long summer days of natural light, instead of using unnecessary electricity.

There is no excuse for not following these tips. After all, they are completely free.

a. High temperatures can be responsible for increased energy consumption. ☐

b. The position of air conditioning units in the home is not important. ☐

c. You do not need to turn on fans 10 minutes before using them. ☐

d. Using a barbecue is often a way of saving energy. ☐

e. Being outside is a way of saving energy. ☐

f. All of the tips are inexpensive to follow. ☐

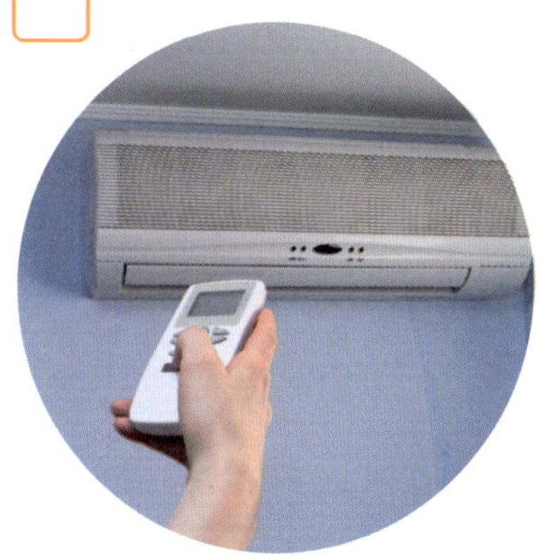

11 Read the text in Activity 10 again and circle five key words. Write them down.

____

____

12 Choose two words from Activity 11 and write a sentence with each of them.

a. ____

b. ____

UNIT 8 Electricity and magnetism

1 Read the sentences about magnets and decide whether they are true (**T**) or false (**F**).

a. The area of force produced by a magnet is called a magnetic field. ☐

b. Metals are not attracted to magnets. ☐

c. The Earth has its own magnetic field. ☐

d. A compass uses the Earth's magnetic field for directions. ☐

e. Magnetic fields are visible to the human eye. ☐

f. Induced magnets never lose their magnetism. ☐

g. Electromagnets are used in speakers, hairdryers and glasses. ☐

2 Decide which household item with magnets is being described. Use the items from the box. There are some extra items.

a stereo	a vacuum cleaner	a hairdryer	a key card	speakers

a. This item plays radio or cd music and has magnets in its speaker parts. The magnetic forces make the speakers vibrate.

____

b. This item's electric motor is powered by magnetism. The forces make the motor spin and suck up other items from the floor.

____

c. This device consists of a magnetic strip that opens a door.

____

3 Label the photos with words from Activity 2.

a

____

b

____

c

____

4 Tick (✔) the objects that use magnets.

a. a hairdryer ☐
b. a key made out of iron ☐
c. a coin ☐
d. speakers ☐
e. a paper clip ☐
f. a microphone ☐
g. a hard disk ☐
h. a pen ☐
i. a credit card ☐
j. a silver ring ☐
k. an MRI scanner ☐
l. a CD ☐

5 Identify the mistakes in the following sentences and correct them.

a. Benjamin Franklin lived in the 20th century.

____

b. He founded the first public hospital in the USA.

____

c. He experimented with magnetism.

____

d. He carried out an experiment to find out if thunder was a form of electricity.

____

e. In this experiment, he used a ball and a Leyden jar.

____

f. Franklin invented a Leyden jar which protects buildings from lightning strikes.

____

6 Imagine you are Benjamin Franklin and you have just discovered lightning is electricity. Give an account of what you experienced that day. How do you feel? What have you discovered exactly? Why might it be so important to know about it?

____

____

____

____

7 Answer the questions.

a. Where was Hans Christian Ørsted from?

b. What did he research?

c. What did he discover?

d. What is an oersted?

8 Write definitions for the following terms.

a. atom:

b. electron:

c. proton:

d. static electricity:

e. electromagnet:

9 Tick (✔) the objects that are attracted to magnets.

a. a silver coin ☐
b. a plastic cup ☐
c. a wooden pencil ☐
d. iron filings ☐
e. a gold ring ☐
f. a rubber ☐
g. a piece of paper ☐
h. a glass vase ☐
i. a bookmark made of steel ☐
j. iron nails ☐
k. matches ☐
l. a leather belt ☐

10 Label the parts of the electromagnet. Explain how it works.

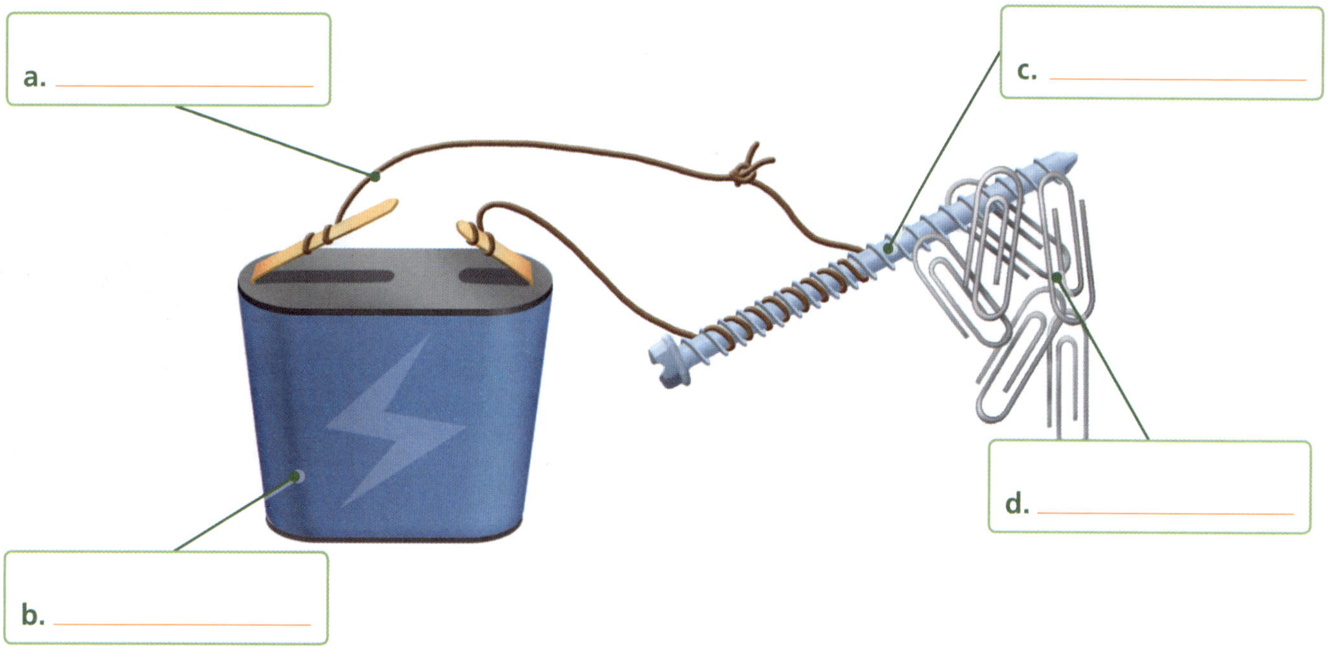

______

______

11 Choose the correct word to complete each sentence.

1. Electromagnets are ______ for a lot of things.

   a. use **b.** not used **c.** used

2. Hans Christian Ørsted first connected a battery ______ a wire.

   a. from **b.** around **c.** to

3. Hairdryers, microphones and hard disks ______ use magnets.

   a. each one **b.** all **c.** all of

4. In the 1800s, Michael Faraday showed that magnetism ______ produce electricity.

   a. could **b.** can **c.** must

12 List 10 objects that you use every day that contain magnets.

______

______

______

Project work

13 How do you think people in the past lived without electricity? Do you know any groups of people who do not use electricity as part of their culture?

Method

1. Think about everything you do on a Saturday or Sunday that involves electricity, for example *watching TV.* Write a list. There are many!
2. Think about all the things you could do without using electricity. Write a list of alternative electricity-free things to do, for example *reading a book*.
3. Find out what some Amish people do instead of using electricity. Take some more ideas from them.
4. See how long you can last without electricity. You could even turn it into a competition with a friend or family member.

activities that involve electricity	electricity-free activities	typical Amish activities

Conclusions

1. How long did you last without electricity?

2. Did you enjoy your electricity-free alternatives? Why (not)?

3. How would it make you feel if you had to live without electricity like some Amish people do?

Skills check

14 Choose the correct option to complete each sentence.

a. You *should / don't have to / mustn't* take care when using electricity.
b. You *don't have to / mustn't / shouldn't* use electrical appliances that are wet.
c. You *can't / should / mustn't* call an electrician if you have any problems with electricity at home.
d. You *don't have to / should / mustn't* put anything into a socket other than a plug.
e. You *shouldn't / don't have to / can* overload sockets and extension leads.

15 Write a letter.

This is part of a letter you received from a friend at another school. Write a short answer to your friend.
We are doing a project on the dangers of electricity in our homes. I'm finding it difficult. What do you think we should write about?

Tips

1. It's an informal letter so use contractions.
2. Organise your letter into clear paragraphs and use phrases such as:
   - Thanks for your letter.
   - It's great to hear from you.
   - Anyway, I'm going to help you with ...
   - I look forward to hearing from you again soon.

Dear ______________________

UNIT 9 Using technology

1 **Read the text about how technology has changed our homes. Then answer the questions.**

Technological advances have changed our homes dramatically. They have changed the way we live, work, play and generally interact. Wireless phones mean we can move about while we talk, surround sound systems mean we can watch a film as if we were in the cinema and improved Internet access means we can work from home. Technology means we can juggle the demands of work with other things in our lives, such as leisure time and entertainment. However, we should not forget that there are of course some disadvantages to having such sophisticated equipment in our lives.

a. Which word means 'using a system of radio signals rather than cables to connect devices to each other'?

b. Which word means 'to do several things at the same time'?

c. What do you think the disadvantages of technology are?

d. Do you think everyone in the world has access to such technology? Why do you think this is?

2 **Read about three items of technology. What is the name of each of them? Which area of life does each one belong to: transport, education or medicine?**

a. This is a biological product that stimulates the body's immune system.

b. This is a technological device that is used to aid learning and makes learning more tactile and entertaining.

c. This is a train that uses magnetic levitation to hover above the track.

3 Read about schools in the 1950s and schools in the 21st century. Write sentences comparing them below.

Classroom technologies have developed a lot and they are becoming more and more sophisticated as the years go by. In the 1950s, the teacher would use a blackboard with chalk but now we have interactive whiteboards, so the students can participate more actively. There was no Internet in the 1950s, so students had to use encyclopaedias and the library for their research and homework. Students in the 1950s learnt subjects like Science, Maths and English, whereas students in the 21st century can choose from a greater variety of subjects including Citizenship, and Art and Design.

1. sophistication: *Old classrooms were less sophisticated than 21st century classrooms.*
2. participation: ______
3. homework: ______
4. subjects: ______

4 If you could choose, would you prefer to live in a time before the invention of smartphones? Make a list of the advantages and disadvantages of living before smartphones were invented.

Advantages:

Fewer distractions – I could concentrate on my work without people bothering me via instant messaging.

✔ ______

✔ ______

✔ ______

✔ ______

Disadvantages:

✗ ______

✗ ______

✗ ______

✗ ______

5 Classify the items according to the aspect of life they relate to. Some items can be used more than once. Add two examples of your own to each category.

tablet computer	vaccine	interactive whiteboard	smartphone	3D printer
washing machine	aeroplane	organ transplant	smart glasses	laptop
laser surgery	high-speed train	USB flash drive	underground train systems	

education	medicine	transport	communication	home

6 What is your opinion of 3D printers? Write about their advantages and disadvantages. You can give both personal and general answers.

Opinion:

Advantages:

Disadvantages:

7 Think about computers and the Internet. Then, write a factual sentence about each given topic.

a. YouTube

b. malware

c. mouse

d. Google

e. blog

f. Internet browser

g. Facebook

8 Imagine you are going to give a presentation on the problems associated with using social media websites such as Facebook, Twitter and LinkedIn. What do you think the problems are? What would you tell people to be wary of? Make notes.

Project work

9 Answer the questions.

a. What are blogs? ______________________________

____

____

b. What do people use blogs for? ______________________________

____

____

c. Do you think they are a good idea? Why? ______________________________

____

____

d. Do you have a blog? If so, what is it about? If not, do you know any websites that assist you with making a blog?

____

____

10 You are going to create a blog about technology.

Method

1. Sign up to a free blog site like WordPress or any other one that you like the look of.
2. Enter your email address, a blog name (something related to the topic) and a password. Make sure these details are secure and that you and no one else knows them.
3. Think about the answers to the following questions for ideas for your technology blog:
   - **a.** What's the latest piece of technology?
   - **b.** What's your favourite gadget?
   - **c.** What gadgets do you not like?
   - **d.** What was your favourite gadget last month?
4. Write your answers to these questions and post them on your blog.
5. Add to this blog every month answering the same questions and other ones that you think of.

Extra questions to answer:

- What do you think the dangers of having too many gadgets are?
- Do you know anyone who doesn't own any type of electronic gadget such as a laptop, tablet computer or smartphone? What are the pros and cons of not owning any of these gadgets?
- Do you think technological advances are always positive? Why (not)?

Skills check

11 Read the text about the Internet. Then decide if the sentences below are true or false.

The World Wide Web was first launched in 1991. Within four years, it had about 50 million users. However, it took the television 13 years to achieve the same user numbers. Nowadays, web browsers such as Mozilla Firefox and Google Chrome are popular, but in the beginning, the most popular one was Mosaic. This browser was used from 1993 to 1997. This is not the only aspect that has changed about the Internet. Every year the Internet changes its design; you only have to look at Google as an example. Social networking websites also undergo drastic and continual changes. Facebook, for example, looked very different when it was first launched. People who use such websites have been predicted to spend about 10 per cent of their entire lifetime using them. Isn't that scary? This brings us to the disadvantages of such advancements in technology. It is not just an addiction to technology that we have to be careful of. It is also very important to stay safe online. It may be a 'virtual' world, but the Internet has its own hidden dangers. People can even be attacked online. What do we mean by the word 'attacked'? If a person does not keep their computer and Internet protected, they face the possibility of becoming the victim of a cybercrime such as identity theft or bullying.

a. It took the television eight more years than the Internet to accrue 50 million users. ☐

b. Mosaic was around for three years. ☐

c. Google changes its design every six months. ☐

d. People don't spend enough time on social media websites. ☐

e. The only danger that the Internet has is cybercrime. ☐

12 What should we do to be safe on the Internet? List at least five things.

Glossary

English	Your language

Unit 1: Interaction

English	Your language
bitter (adj)	
brain (n)	
brain stem (n)	
calf muscle (n)	
cartilage (n)	
cerebellum (n)	
cerebrum (n)	
chest (n)	
clavicle (n)	
cochlea (n)	
comprise (v)	
cornea (n)	
cranium (n)	
decline (v)	
deltoid (n)	
dermis (n)	
detect (v)	
eardrum (n)	
flavour (n)	
fragrance (n)	
gluteus (n)	
hemisphere (n)	
humerus (n)	
iris (n)	
joint (n)	
lens (n)	
ligament (n)	
nerve (n)	
neuron (n)	
patella (n)	
pelvis (n)	
pupil (n)	
radius (n)	
retina (n)	
salty (adj)	
scapula (n)	
sour (adj)	
spinal cord (n)	
sternum (n)	
stimulate (v)	
sweet (adj)	
taste buds (n)	
tibia (n)	
transmit (v)	
vital (adj)	

English	Your language	English	Your language

Unit 2: Nutrition

English	Your language	English	Your language
addictive (adj)		lung (n)	
alveolus (n)		oesophagus (n)	
anus (n)		oxygen (n)	
artery (n)		pancreas (n)	
atrium (n)		plasma (n)	
bile (n)		platelet (n)	
bladder (n)		pore (n)	
blood (n)		rectum (n)	
breathe (v)		red blood cell (n)	
bronchiole (n)			
bronchus (n)		stomach (n)	
capillary (n)		substance (n)	
carbon dioxide (n)		supply (v)	
		sweat (v)	
circulation (n)		trachea (n)	
diaphragm (n)		ureter (n)	
digestion (n)		urethra (n)	
drug (n)		urine (n)	
excrete (v)		valve (n)	
exhale (v)		vein (n)	
inhale (v)		ventricle (n)	
intestine (n)		waste (n)	
kidney (n)		white blood cell (n)	
liver (n)			

Glossary

Unit 3: Reproduction

English	Your language
adolescent (n)	
age (v)	
constrict (v)	
dementia (n)	
dilate (v)	
disorder (n)	
ejaculate (v)	
elderly (adj)	
embryo (n)	
fallopian tube (n)	
fertilisation (n)	
fertilise (v)	
foetus (n)	
foundation (n)	
fraternal twins (n)	
gene (n)	
headquarters (n)	
hips (n)	
house (v)	
identical twins (n)	
life expectancy (n)	
menopause (n)	

English	Your language
menstruation (n)	
navel (n)	
ovary (n)	
ovulation (n)	
ovum (n)	
penis (n)	
placenta (n)	
pregnancy (n)	
pregnant (adj)	
prostate (n)	
puberty (n)	
scrotum (n)	
semen (n)	
sperm (n)	
stage (n)	
substantial (adj)	
testicles (n)	
testosterone (n)	
toddler (n)	
umbilical cord (n)	
uterus (n)	
vagina (n)	
zygote (n)	

English	Your language	English	Your language

Unit 4: Living things

English	Your language	English	Your language
algae (n)		invade (v)	
amoeba (n)		invertebrate (n)	
amphibian (n)		mammal (n)	
ancestor (n)		moss (n)	
angiosperm (n)		multicellular (adj)	
animal cell (n)		mushroom (n)	
bird (n)		non-flowering (adj)	
cell membrane (n)		nucleus (n)	
cell wall (n)		organelle (n)	
chlorophyll (n)		parasitic (adj)	
chloroplast (n)		plant cell (n)	
complex (adj)		poisonous (adj)	
controversy (n)		prokaryotic (adj)	
cytoplasm (n)		reptile (n)	
decomposition (n)		seeds (n)	
eukaryotic (adj)		species (n)	
extinction (n)		spores (n)	
fern (n)		stimulus (n)	
fish (n)		tissue (n)	
flourish (v)		unicellular (adj)	
flowering (adj)		vacuole (n)	
fungus (n)		vertebrate (n)	
gymnosperm (n)		virus (n)	
host (n)		yeast (n)	

Glossary

Unit 5: Ecosystems

English	Your language
biodiversity (n)	
biomass (n)	
canopy layer (n)	
carnivore (n)	
community (n)	
decomposer (n)	
desert (n)	
ecological niche (n)	
ecosystem (n)	
emergent layer (n)	
endangered (adj)	
extinct (adj)	
flourish (v)	
food chain (n)	
food web (n)	
forest floor (n)	
grassland (n)	

English	Your language
habitat (n)	
herbivore (n)	
hunt (v)	
inhabit (v)	
loss (n)	
omnivore (n)	
pigeon (n)	
population (n)	
predator (n)	
prey (n)	
primary consumer (n)	
producer (n)	
secondary consumer (n)	
sparrow (n)	
temperate forest (n)	
tertiary consumer (n)	
tropical rainforest (n)	
tundra (n)	
understory layer (n)	

English	Your language	English	Your language

Unit 6: Matter

English	Your language	English	Your language
abundant (adj)		heat (n)	
antiseptic (adj)		heterogeneous (adj)	
boil (v)		homogeneous (adj)	
burn (v)		lactose (n)	
chemical change (n)		magnetic separation (n)	
chlorine (n)		matter (n)	
combustion (n)		mineral (n)	
component (n)		mixture (n)	
decant (v)		oxidation (n)	
decantation (n)		particles (n)	
dehydrate (v)		property (n)	
density (n)		pure substance (n)	
desalinate (v)			
desalination (n)		react (v)	
distillation (n)		regulate (v)	
evaporation (n)		remove (v)	
extract (v)		rust (n)	
fermentation (n)		seawater (n)	
filtration (n)			
float (v)		sediment (n)	
fructose (n)		stainless steel (n)	
fuel (n)			
glucose (n)		yeast (n)	

Glossary

English	Your language

Unit 7: Energy

acid rain (n)

biomass (n)

chemical energy (n)

coal (n)

conduction (n)

convection (n)

decibel (n)

electrical energy (n)

fossil fuel (n)

global warming (n)

greenhouse effect (n)

heat energy (n)

kinetic energy (n)

lens (n)

light energy (n)

mass (n)

mechanical energy (n)

mirror (n)

non-renewable (adj)

opaque (adj)

potential energy (n)

radiation (n)

radioactive (adj)

reflection (n)

refraction (n)

renewable (adj)

sound energy (n)

thermal conductor (n)

thermal insulator (n)

translucent (adj)

transparent (adj)

volume (n)

wind farm (n)

English	Your language	English	Your language

Unit 8: Electricity and magnetism

English	Your language	English	Your language
angle (n)		fuse box (n)	
atom (n)		headphones (n)	
attraction (n)		induced magnet (n)	
battery (n)			
cardinal point (n)		iron (n)	
		lightning (n)	
circuit (n)		magnet (n)	
coil (n)		magnetic field (n)	
compass (n)			
conduct (v)		magnetism (n)	
conductor (n)		magnetite (n)	
copper (n)		permanent magnet (n)	
core (n)			
discover (v)		pole (n)	
door latch (n)		proton (n)	
electric shock (n)		rely (v)	
		repel (v)	
electrical appliance (n)		socket (n)	
		speakers (n)	
electrical current (n)		spin (v)	
electrician (n)		switch on (v)	
electricity (n)		switch off (v)	
electromagnet (n)		visible (adj)	
electron (n)		wire (n)	

Glossary

English	Your language	English	Your language

Unit 9: Using technology

English	Your language
3D printer (n)	
advancement (n)	
application (n)	
astounding (adj)	
blog (n)	
browser (n)	
bullying (n)	
chalk (n)	
cybercrime (n)	
device (n)	
drastic (adj)	
drawbacks (n)	
gadget (n)	
hardware (n)	
high-speed train (n)	
hover (v)	
identity theft (n)	
interact (v)	
interactive whiteboard (n)	
juggle (v)	
laptop (n)	
launch (v)	
keyboard (n)	
laptop (n)	
malware (n)	
pacemaker (n)	
password (n)	
printer (n)	
printing press (n)	
procedure (n)	
router (n)	
search engine (n)	
server (n)	
social media (n)	
software (n)	
sophisticated (adj)	
speaker (n)	
tactile (adj)	
touchpad (n)	
transplant (n)	
USB flash drive (n)	
victim (n)	
wiki (n)	
wireless (adj)	